Revelation

Revelation

Poems by

Nancy Dillingham

© 2019 Nancy Dillingham. All rights reserved.
This material may not be reproduced in any form, published,
reprinted, recorded, performed, broadcast,
rewritten or redistributed without
the explicit permission of Nancy Dillingham.
All such actions are strictly prohibited by law.

Cover design by Shay Culligan
Cover art by Olga Dorenko
"A Part of the Whole," oil on canvas

ISBN: 978-1-950462-43-8

Kelsay Books Inc.

kelsaybooks.com

502 S 1040 E. A119
American Fork, Utah 84003

Contents

Advent 2017

Magi	13
Starshine	14
Mary's Lament	15
Babe in Bethlehem	16

Lenten 2018

Lenten Lily	19
Journey to Golgotha	20
At the Tomb	21

Advent 2018

Seeking the Divine	25
Come, Peace	26
Christmas Round	27
Burning the Greens	28

Lent 2019

Promise	31
Golgotha	32
Prophecy	33
Forerunner	34
Journey	35
Gethsemane	36
The Light	37

The soul should always stand ajar,
ready to welcome the ecstatic experience.
—Emily Dickinson

Advent 2017

Magi

Sparked by a star
armed with a prophecy
and astronomical knowledge

wise men on camels
bearing gifts of gold
frankincense and myrrh

traveled cold terrain
certain of their journey

At darkness or dawn
purple-ribboned horizons
foretold the royalty they sought

Undeterred by stranger
omens or danger
they pressed onward

spurred by faith
and the promise of a miracle
in a manger

Starshine

Brighter than any light
that might have emanated
from a fire

in the center
of their sleeping stones
the star shone

streaming high above them
pulsating
awakening them

Those dozing
may have thought
they were dreaming the voice

as it intoned a command
same as the one
they might have given their flock

enticing them to the fold
guiding them
inviting them to arise and go

and follow starshine
to a destiny
on the plain

Mary's Lament

An ominous heaviness
hangs over me
I stifle the urge to flee

Not easily
I suffer the weight
of my husband's glances

Real or imagined
I wonder about his chances
of leaving me

The distance
between us
seems a wide and silent sea

I plea
for some measured
degree of faith

Still as I wait
a seed grows
within me

I breathe a Savior

Babe in Bethlehem

In the silence of a stable
a baby lies in a manger
haloed in swaddling clothes

the air acrid
raw with the smell
of animal and straw

Mary the mother hovers
Joseph her husband
steady and strong

the whole tableau
fraught with awe
a Savior come calling

Lenten 2018

Lenten Lily

Believed to bloom in the braces
between Ash Wednesday and Easter

wild daffodils erase
covering earth's ugliness

their trumpet faces
announcing Christ's coming

their golden color
reminder of sunshine

the brightness of spring
the worth of rebirth

Journey to Golgotha

See his mother weeping
recoiling in disbelief

as her son confronts
his suffering

Hear the cacophony
of the crowds

Follow the throng
hear their taunts

See Simon
shoulder his load

when he falters
on the dusty road

Watch soldiers nail his feet
Feel the pierce in his side

Be the thief
beside him

as he dies
in the darkening skies

when he rises
in paradise

At the Tomb

In pre-dawn light
women bearing spices
move in silence to the tomb
cradling their savior
find the stone rolled away
and an empty grave

Entertain a surreal invitation
from a young stranger
who invites them to see that the place
where they laid him is vacant
that he is "not here" but is risen

And later Mary Magdalene
standing in our place
returns weeping
sees the gardener
who call her by name
believes and says "teacher"

Advent 2018

Seeking the Divine

As Jesus
when only a boy
with a yearning
and a thirst

first searched out teachers
in the temple
for answers to the unknown

may we on our own
green hill of hope
seek our truth, our destiny
the journey he bequeathed us

Come, Peace

In a world marred
by bitterness and strife
and the apartheid
of loneliness
we long for
the profundity
of wholeness

an increased awareness
of the power
that marches before us

that encroaches upon
and erodes our hard shell
of indifference

leaves us soft
and vulnerable
ready to accept
the white dove

alighting on our shoulder

Christmas Round

Sweet angels' song
sweet soothing sounds
low holy tones
God comes round

Lowly creatures' moans
shepherds hovering over
humble Mary mother
son Jesus' lovely coming

Burning the Greens

On the coldest
darkest night
of the year

we heap
our greens
onto the hearth

toss them
into the fire
feel its glow

Midst the warmth
our hope
is rekindled

our faith restored
our soul transformed
our rebirth forged

Lent 2019

Promise

The Son
that sprung
from Jesse's seed

that stuck
His oar
into the water

that moved
through the sea

that stunned
the Pharisees

that gathered
disciples
like waves

saved multitudes
turned water
into wine

still waits
on the shoreline
in our time

Golgotha

At that place
they mocked you
spat on you

set a crown of thorns
on your head
called you King of the Jews

nailed you to the cross
offered you gall to drink
cast lots for your robe

ran a spear
through your side
crucified you

A pall fell
the earth quaked
the sky turned dark

rocks split
tombs broke open

As your head sank
upon your chest
you cried out

and prayed
Father, forgive them
for they know not what they do

Prophecy

At the Place
of the Skull

Mary his mother
sees her baby's face
in the stable

feels the strangeness
in the temple
that day

remembers
her puzzlement
as Simon proclaimed

that her son
was "anointed
for the falling"

And as she takes
in the appalling truth
and feels the pain

of her son's fate
she remembers
the prophecy

that she will feel
as if she were run through
by a long stake

Forerunner

His birth and purpose
proclaimed by the angel Gabriel
John the Baptist
honored God's calling

A prophetic voice
crying in the desert
he became the paradigm
for Christ's life

foretelling His forty days
and nights in the wilds
preparing the way
for His sacrifice

Journey

During the week
of upheaval and strife
leading to his crucifixion

Jesus rode triumphant
into Jerusalem
on a lowly donkey

People lined the streets
with their own garments
cut rushes in his path

waved fronds of palms
symbol of peace
and eternal life

Gethsemane

In the garden
before betrayal and death
Jesus prayed
sweat drops of blood

while three disciples
Peter, John, and James
a stone's throw away
lonely and cold

fell asleep
keeping watch
over the longest night
of the soul

The Light

Dogwoods dotting
the mountainside
remind us of legend

four-petaled
the shape of their blossoms
recalls the cross

their puckered edges
the stigmata
their knotted centers
the clotted crown of thorns

their pure white light
the promise of new life

About the Author

Nancy Dillingham is the author of twelve books of poetry and short fiction and the co-editor of four anthologies of women's writing. Her collection of poems *Home* was nominated for a Southern Independent Booksellers' Alliance Award (SIBA). Her latest book is *Like Headlines: New and Selected Poems*. She lives in Asheville, NC.

www.ingramcontent.com/pod-product-compliance
Lightning Source LLC
Chambersburg PA
CBHW021029090426
42738CB00007B/948